Tip, Pat and Tap

By Sally Cowan

I tip it.

Tip, tip, tip.

I pat it.

Pat, pat, pat.

I tip and tap it.

Tap, tap, tap.

I tip, pat and tap!

CHECKING FOR MEANING

1. What is tipped into the bowl? *(Literal)*

2. What happens at the end of the book? *(Literal)*

3. If the story continued for another page, what do you think would happen? *(Inferential)*

EXTENDING VOCABULARY

tap	Look at the word *tap*. What sounds are in this word? Which sound is changed to turn *tap* into *tip*?
pat	Look at the word *pat*. What smaller word is at the end of *pat*? What other words do you know that rhyme with *pat*?
tip	Look at the word *tip* and think about what it means in the story. Can you think of another word that means the same as *tip*?

MOVING BEYOND THE TEXT

1. What do you have to be careful of when you are baking?

2. What are your favourite things to bake or cook?

3. What kinds of foods are baked in an oven?

4. What are some healthy things to eat?

SPEED SOUNDS

Mm	Ss	Aa	Pp	Ii	Tt

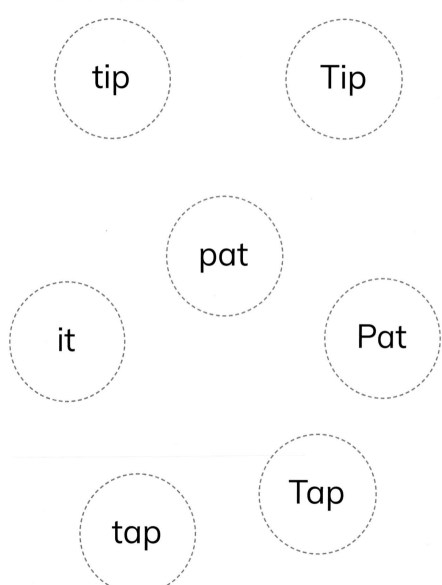

tip

Tip

pat

it

Pat

Tap

tap